DATE DUE

AID	OCT 26	=
ADH	NOV 19	
McDonald		
McDonald		
GR3		
BLH	DEC 11	
REG	JAN 25	
VGH	APR 2 3	
ACH	MAY 3 0	
VCI	MAR 0 8	
ESH	MAR 1 7	
DRE	MAR 2 5	
SSJ	MAY 2 4	

DEMCO 38-297

What's Inside the Ocean?

Jane Kelly Kosek

The Rosen Publishing Group's
PowerKids Press™
New York

For Karen and Jim—may your relationship hold as many treasures as the ocean.
Special thanks to Christopher H. Starr at the Pacific-Sierra Research Corporation.

Published in 1999 by The Rosen Publishing Group, Inc.
29 East 21st Street, New York, NY 10010

First Edition

Book Design: Kim Sonsky

Photo Credits: Cover, title page © Color Box/FPG International; Contents page, p. 10 © PhotoDisc; pp. 5, 9, 14 © Telegraph Colour Library/FPG International; p. 6 Frederick McKinney/FPG International; p. 9 © Travel pix/FPG International; p. 13 Chad Ehlers/International Stock; p. 15 © David Fleetham/FPG International; p. 15 © Roger Markham Smith/International Stock; p. 17 © Ben Waddle/Midwest Stock; p. 18 © Elliott Warner Smith/International Stock; p. 20 R. Rathe/FPG International; p. 21 © Victor Alemen/FPG International; p. 21 © Ron Church/FPG International.

Kosek, Jane Kelly.
    What's inside the ocean? / by Jane Kelly Kosek.
        p.   cm. — (The what's inside library)
    Includes index.
    Summary: Discusses some of the life forms that live in the ocean, such as the coral polyp, phytoplankton, and the great blue whale, and explains how they survive.
    ISBN 0-8239-5278-9
    1. Marine biology—Juvenile literature. [1. Marine biology.]
    I. Title. II. Series: Kosek, Jane Kelly. What's inside library.
QH91.16.K67 1998
578.77—dc21   98–11743
                                                                            CIP
                                                                            AC

Manufactured in the United States of America

Contents

A Watery Planet

The ocean covers about 3/4 of our planet Earth. It is made up of five separate oceans: the Antarctic, Arctic, Atlantic, Indian, and Pacific. The ocean can be divided into even smaller bodies of water, such as bays, gulfs, and seas. Ocean water is called salt water because it contains a lot of salt.

Most of the living things on Earth live in the ocean. There are three main areas of the ocean where life is found—near the coast, at the surface, and at the bottom of the ocean. The largest animal on Earth lives in the ocean. It is the blue whale, which can weigh up to 300,000 pounds!

Whales, such as the blue whale, are found in all the oceans of the world. ▶

Living in Water

We move on land by walking with our legs. Ocean animals move in the water by either swimming or floating. Their bodies are shaped to move easily through water. You may have noticed that it's harder to move in water than move on land. This is because water is **denser** (DEN-ser) than air.

Ocean animals also feel the **pressure** (PREH-sher) of the water. As they go deeper into the ocean, the weight of the water increases. This causes the pressure of the water to increase as well. Creatures at the bottom of the ocean live under 1,000 times more pressure than those at the surface. Also, sunlight only reaches 3,300 feet into the ocean. This makes the ocean dark and cold as you dive deeper.

We aren't born knowing how to swim, like fish and some animals. We have to learn how to swim.

Places to Live

Most marine life, or plants and animals in the ocean, are found in shallow water. Many different kinds of ocean creatures live together in a **coral reef** (KOR-ul REEF), which is made of **coral polyps** (KOR-ul PO-lyps). A coral polyp likes warm, shallow salt water. When a coral polyp dies, it becomes a base on which another polyp can attach itself and live. As more and more polyps grow on top of each other and then die, coral reefs are created. At 1,250 miles long, the Great Barrier Reef off the coast of Australia is the longest coral reef in the world.

Marine life is also found along the shallow waters of the coast, where the water meets the land. Here plants and animals live on rocky shores, sandy beaches, or in **wetlands** (WET-landz). Marine life is also found along the large and cold ocean floor.

Reefs, such as the Great Barrier Reef (top photo), are homes to different kinds of ocean life, such as the lion fish.

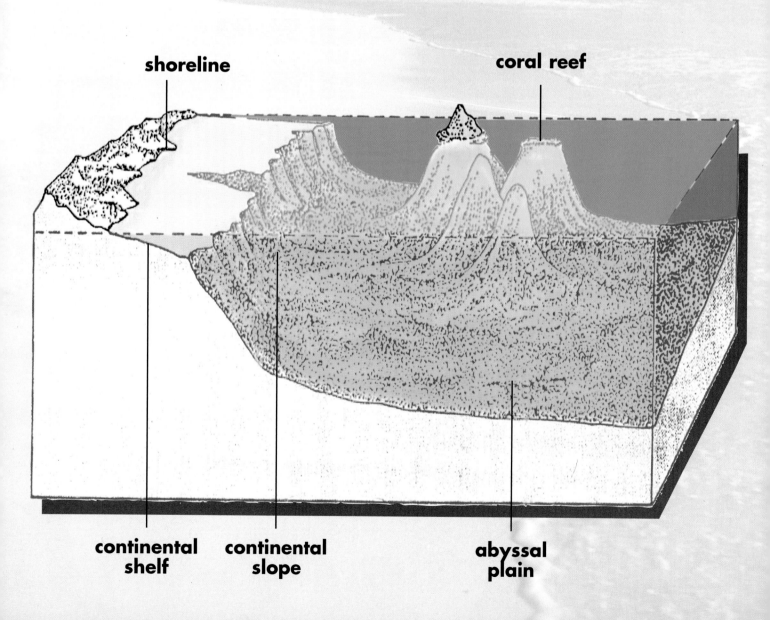

shoreline

coral reef

continental shelf

continental slope

abyssal plain

The Ocean Floor

When you step into the ocean, you are standing on part of the ocean floor, or the **continental shelf** (KON-tih-NEN-tul SHELF). This shelf slopes downward until it reaches a drop called the **continental slope** (KON-tih-NEN-tul SLOHP.) The slope drops down about 2.5 miles to the ocean basin. The ocean basin is mainly made up of flat areas, called **abyssal plains** (uh-BIS-ul PLAYNZ). It also has mountains, **volcanoes** (vol-KAY-nohz), and deep **trenches** (TREN-chez).

The largest mountain range is the Mid-Atlantic Ridge that runs through the middle of the Atlantic Ocean. The Pacific Ocean has the deepest trench, called the Marianas Trench. It is 36,198 feet below the ocean's surface.

You'd never know just by looking at the ocean from the beach that below the water's surface is a maze of mountains and trenches.

Plants

Ocean plants are found close to the ocean surface where sunlight can reach them. This is because plants need sunlight for energy. One ocean plant, called **phytoplankton** (FY-toh-plank-tun), is made up of only one **cell** (SEL). Many ocean animals, including the large blue whale, eat the tiny phytoplankton.

Other kinds of ocean plants include sea grasses and seaweeds. Sea grasses are the only flowering plants that can live in salt water. Seaweeds are found in different colors. They may be green, brown, or red.

Some sea grass can be found along the ocean's coast, where it washes up with the tide. ▶

Invertebrates

Animals without backbones are called **invertebrates** (in-VER-tuh-brayts). They make up most of the animals in the ocean. The biggest group of invertebrates are the mollusks. A mollusk has a soft body and usually has a shell. Clams, octopuses, snails, and squids are all examples of mollusks.

Another group of invertebrates is the **crustaceans** (krus-TAY-shunz). Crustaceans have hard outer shells, limbs, and **antennas** (an-TEN-uhz). Crustaceans include crabs, lobsters, and shrimps. Corals, **sea anemones** (SEE uh-NEM-oh-neez), and sponges are invertebrates that must attach themselves to hard objects to live.

Sea anemones can look like large colorful flowers waving in the ocean.

15

Fish

Fish spend their whole lives in water. Instead of breathing air, like we do, they use their gills to take **oxygen** (AHK-sih-jin) from the water. Gills are like vents on either side of a fish's body. As water passes over its gills, the fish takes in oxygen and lets the other parts of the water flow through its gills.

Fish are found at all different levels of the ocean. The most colorful fish are found in coral reefs. They use their colors to attract mates in the busy, crowded reef. The strangest looking fish are found on the ocean's floor. There isn't much food to eat deep in the ocean, so what they do eat has to last for a while. Because of this, these fish often have big mouths and stretchy stomachs that hold a lot of food at once. They usually eat dead plants or animals that have floated down from the surface.

The rockfish lives among the reefs and rocky areas of the ocean. ▶

The seal uses its
strong flippers
not only to swim
in cold ocean
waters but also
to walk on land.

Mammals and Reptiles

Marine **mammals** (MAM-mulz) and **reptiles** (REP-tylz) live in the ocean but they don't have gills like fish. They need air to breathe. These animals can stay underwater longer than humans can. Some can stay underwater for more than thirty minutes.

Marine mammals have a layer of fat called blubber to keep them warm. They give birth to live young and feed them milk from their bodies. They move their tails up and down or back and forth in order to swim, and teach their young to do the same. Marine mammals include dolphins, seals, walruses, and whales.

Ocean reptiles include iguanas, sea snakes, and turtles. Most reptiles hatch from eggs on land and then make their way to the water. Reptiles usually live in spots that are warm, and they lie in the sun to warm themselves.

Working Underwater

Scientists need ways to study the ocean, but they don't want to come up for air every few minutes. To solve this problem, they invented the **submersible** (sub-MER-sih-bul). The first submersible was built in 1959 by an ocean explorer named Jacques Cousteau. Since then, submersibles have been used to study things such as marine life, shipwrecks, and the bottom of the ocean. To study for long periods of time, they built the only undersea laboratory in the world, called the *Aquarius*.

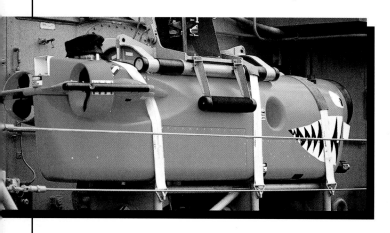

It is about 65 feet below the ocean's surface near Key Largo, Florida. Scientists usually go down to the laboratory for two weeks at a time and study.

Jacques Cousteau called his submersible a "diving saucer." It could dive up to 1,000 feet and hold three passengers. ▶ Another submersible can be seen at left.

Looking Ahead

Each area in the ocean holds different plants and animals. But these plants and animals are threatened every day by pollution. Oil spills and **chemicals** (KEM-ih-kulz) dumped into the ocean have killed many plants and animals in the ocean and on land. Dolphins and other marine life are dying from getting caught in fishing nets that are left in the ocean.

We can help protect the ocean by cleaning up after ourselves when we go to the beach. At home we learn how to recycle. It is important to take care of the ocean. We still have more to learn about what's inside it.

Web Site:

To find out more about the ocean, check out this Web site:
http://oceanlink.island.net

Glossary

abyssal plain (uh-BIS-ul PLAYN) A flat area on the bottom of the ocean.

antenna (an-TEN-uh) A thin, rod-like organ on the head of a crustacean that it uses to feel things around it.

cell (SEL) The basic building block of all living things.

chemical (KEM-ih-kul) Something that is dangerous to the ocean if not disposed of properly.

continental shelf (KON-tih-NEN-tul SHELF) A flat, shallow part of the ocean floor that begins where the land meets the water and ends at a continental slope.

continental slope (KON-tih-NEN-tul SLOHP) A steep drop from a continental shelf to the bottom of the ocean.

coral polyp (KOR-ul PO-lyp) A small ocean animal whose skeleton makes up coral.

coral reef (KOR-ul REEF) A chain of coral where many ocean creatures live.

crustacean (krus-TAY-shun) An invertebrate with a hard shell, limbs, and antennas.

denser (DEN-ser) Thicker.

invertebrate (in-VER-tuh-brayt) An animal without a backbone.

mammal (MAM-mul) An animal that has a backbone and breathes air. It also gives birth to live young and feeds its babies milk from its body.

oxygen (AHK-sih-jin) A colorless gas that many forms of life need to live.

phytoplankton (FY-toh-plank-tun) An ocean plant made up of one cell.

pressure (PREH-sher) The action between two opposing forces.

reptile (REP-tyl) An animal that hatches from an egg and gets its warmth from the sun.

sea anemone (SEE uh-NEM-oh-nee) A colorful ocean animal that looks like a flower.

submersible (sub-MER-sih-bul) A machine in which scientists can study the ocean.

trench (TRENCH) A deep area in the ocean floor.

volcano (vol-KAY-noh) An opening in Earth's crust through which hot, liquid rock is sometimes forced out.

wetland (WET-land) An area of shallow water near the coast where the water moves slowly and many ocean creatures live.

Index